Devotions for Those with Anxiety Disorders, Including Post Traumatic Stress Disorder (PTSD)

Jazz Garrett

iUniverse, Inc.
New York   Bloomington

Devotions for Those with Anxiety Disorders, Including
Post Traumatic Stress Disorder (PTSD)

iUniverse books may be ordered through booksellers or by contacting:

iUniverse
1663 Liberty Drive
Bloomington, IN 47403
www.iuniverse.com
1-800-Authors (1-800-288-4677)

Because of the dynamic nature of the Internet, any Web addresses or links contained in this book
may have changed since publication and may no longer be valid.

All scripture is taken from The Holy Bible, New International Version,
copyright 1973, 1978, 1984 by International Bible Society.

ISBN: 978-1-4502-0573-3 (sc)
ISBN: 978-1-4502-0575-7 (dj)
ISBN: 978-1-4502-0574-0 (ebk)

Printed in the United States of America

iUniverse rev. date: 1/18/2010

Thanks to God for inspiring me and being with me throughout my life.
"Give thanks to the Lord for he is good, his love endures forever." (Ps 107:1)

A special thanks to my husband, Billy Garrett who encourages and supports me and is my best friend.

Introduction

Do you want relief from your symptoms of anxiety disorder? Do you need more control of your symptoms?

This book is based on scripture and offers exercises to help you gain some relief and control in focusing on whole-health wellness. This includes focusing on the mind, body, and spirit. If religion is not a part of your life, you may still benefit from spirituality and some of the spiritual skills described in this book.

The Bible is so relevant today that many of the answers and advice we need are provided inside. It is the best book ever written and none other can compare. Trust in God, read the Bible and see what answers you find. If you find a verse that talks to you, write it down on an index card and carry it with you in your purse or billfold.

I wrote this book as a result of my own search for living with PTSD and depression. I wanted to share my insights with others in hope of contributing to and promoting whole-health wellness.

Each devotion contains a scripture passage and exercises. I recommend you spend meditation time on the scriptures each day before reading the section and completing the exercises.

I am a Licensed Professional Counselor and Certified Traumatologist. I was called to counsel survivors of the Oklahoma City Bombing in 1995and the terrorist attacks of 9-11. For twenty-six months I was in Iraq, Kuwait, and Afghanistan working with traumatized and anxious persons. I have also worked multiple local and national disasters as a Mental Health Supervisor through the Red Cross.

The prevalence of anxiety disorder affects between 20 to 37 percent of the population according to the *Diagnostic and Statistical Manual of Mental Disorders, 4th edition* (DSM IV). This includes acute and chronic disorders. Some of the symptoms include upset stomach, ulcers, muscle tension, headaches, sweating, chest pain, jaw pain, shaking, dizziness, and shortness of breath. Diagnostic symptoms for an anxiety disorder are different for each person, but some similarities between patients include fear, worry and avoidance.

There are twelve anxiety disorders listed in the DSM-IV: Panic Disorder without History of Agoraphobia, Panic Disorder with Agoraphobia, Agoraphobia without History of Panic Disorder, Specific Phobia, Social Phobia, Obsessive-Compulsion Disorder, Post-traumatic Stress Disorder, Acute Stress Disorder, Generalized Anxiety Disorder, Anxiety Disorder Due to a General Medical Condition, Substance-Induced Anxiety Disorder and Anxiety Disorder Not Otherwise Specified.

You may have Panic Disorder with other Anxiety Disorders including, but not limited to; Agoraphobia, Social Phobia, Specific Phobia, Post-traumatic Stress Disorder, or Acute Stress Disorder. In addition, you may have another disorder associated with Anxiety Disorder, including most common Depression and Substance Abuse Disorder.

Therapy and medications are commonly used to treat anxiety disorders, and if you are currently on medication or therapy, continue with this regime and use this book as an adjunct. Today a wide range of treatment modalities are being researched some with very good results. Exercise, biofeedback, Yoga (Sheryl Walters 2009), Eye Movement Desensitization Reprocessing (EMDR) – Francine Shapiro, meditation, and mindfulness (Brantley and Millstine 2008) have been getting good research reviews. A new aspect in the counseling profession is using a person's'- religion in therapy, and research has demonstrated that the outcome of that therapy is improved (American Counseling Association).

Virtual Reality games are being researched for combat veterans, and the research thus far has been promising, but research has been limited (Figley and Nash 2007). More research is needed to validate the effectiveness.

If you have not already done so, get a physical exam from your doctor to identify any underlying health problems and so that you can know your personal limitations.

Do not stop taking any medications without your doctor's advice and guidance. I also want to stress that if you are in counseling, do not stop, but possibly take some of these interventions in to talk with your therapist. I continue my medication regime and use the interventions with good results; they have lowered my tension, increased my ability to leave the house, decreased my depression (I was able to stop my depression medication), increased my hopefulness, improved my relations with others and God, and reduced the number of panic attacks.

Anxiety not only affects the anxious person, but those we live with or have relationships with. A goal for me with this book is for everyone to have someone to talk with that they trust with the inner most fears; whether that is a counselor, minister, spouse, friend or God. That person will be referred to as your confidant. That takes trust which is difficult with an anxious person. Feeling less isolated in your disorder helps with recovery or stabilization.

Bessel van der Kolk wrote an article called "The Body Keeps Score" in the *Harvard Review of Psychiatry* (1994). He has been a leader in research of treatment modalities for PTSD. I have found this to be true, as my pain is a direct result of the symptoms of my trauma. I developed PTSD in Afghanistan after attacks on the base I was on. Therefore, in order to completely heal one has to focus on the mind, body and spirit.

I use some body work in my exercises in this book, along with the mental and emotional workouts. If any movement in this book causes you pain, stop immediately. If you are a runner or have been in the military some of the stretches and twists will be familiar; stretching and twisting helps to release tension. I recommend doing Yoga in your daily routine; it gets you moving at a controlled and peaceful pace and helps in strengthening and stretching the body while clearing the mind. If you are new to Yoga, start with a beginner's tape. Patience and persistence are required since you will not be used to some of the poses and stretches.

"My God, My God, why have

you forsaken me?"

Matthew 27:46

Taking Stock

In the beginning I felt that God wasn't with me at the time I needed him; otherwise the events leading to my anxiety wouldn't have happened. The verse above is what Jesus asked God on the cross, so in his human form he had doubts. It took me about six months to forgive myself for not trusting that the Lord was with me. I, now, easily relate to those suffering with anxiety.

I am a counselor and an anxiety sufferer and this has made me research methodologies that were not previously used in the counseling field. By my research and understanding how religion plays a major part in treatment I know that God had not forsaken me. The problem was my not focusing on him as part of my treatment. If you have anger at God due to a past event or circumstances in your life, complete the following intervention and maybe you, too, will see that it was a blessing and the response you had at the time may have saved your life. You also may realize the responses or symptoms you have now may seem excessive, but they can lessen.

Since anxiety tends to be pervasive and interferes with one's life, it is important to know when you are at your best and to make the most of those times. I find that early mornings are best for me, so I plan any outings in the morning. That is also when I do Yoga, prayer, and meditation. I also pray as I do household chores, drive, or am waiting for an appointment. I meditate again in the evening.

Write down the things that are better in your life due to your anxiety. I will start the exercise with some of mine to give you examples. Since I can't always cook, I find great pleasure (and so does my husband) when I can prepare a meal and we eat together in enjoyment and thankfulness to God. I have found that my interactions with my family during my good times are always positive, so I never forget to tell them I love them. I have better communication with my husband because I can talk about what is going on with me. I have developed the ability to "step outside myself" and listen more effectively and empathetically to those who come to me with a problem. I have a closer relationship with God and find comfort in my prayer and reading the bible.

During a time of high anxiety it is difficult to find anything positive and life seems fearful. Take it slow. It may take you several days to find something positive. Keep a journal close at hand as ideas may come up through the day or night. You may want to ask those who are going through this with you; what their favorite things about you are when you are having a good hour/ hours or day.

I lift up my eyes to the hills - where does my

help come from?   My help comes from the LORD

the Maker of heaven and earth.   He will not let your

foot slip - he who watches over you and will not slumber;

indeed, he who watches over Israel will neither slumber

nor sleep. The LORD *watches over you - the* LORD *is your*

shade at your right hand; the sun will not harm you by

day, nor the moon by night. The LORD *will keep you from all*

harm - he will watch over your life; the LORD *will watch*

over your coming and going both now and forevermore.

Psalm 121:1-8

Panic Attacks

Day and night, even when you sleep, God does not. He continues to watch over you and sometimes, as described in the poem "Footprints in the Sand", he carries you, which is why you see only one set of foot prints.

Do you ever feel as if a panic attack won't stop or a flashback or fear, or maybe an obsession, no matter how many times you use a compulsion (an event to lessen the obsession). But they eventually do. There is a reprieve; it may be brief, but there is a time you can just breathe. That reprieve comes from God. He will never give us more than we can handle and he knows our limits even when we do not. It is a comfort to me to know that someone (God), who has more control than I do, is watching over me.

Panic attacks can be frightening. I have had only one which I went to the hospital because of difficulty breathing and pain shooting through my chest. I have been able to control my panic attacks through breathing techniques which I list below for an exercise to lessen the effects.

Breathing is a natural event, but during times of high anxiety just finding your breath is a difficult task. You will need to try different variations to see what works for you.

1. Stand up, pulling your shoulders away from your ears, breathe in through your nose, counting to three. Then breathe out through your nose to a count of three.
2. If you are uncomfortable standing, try sitting upright. Bring your shoulders away from your ears and breathe in through your nose for a count of three, then out again through your nose for a count of three.
3. Continue to complete the rounds of in and out breathing, raising your chest while softening your abdomen. Breathing through your nose with your mouth closed is the most effective. Try to work your way up to a count of six, with a pause between your in breath and your out breath.
4. Never hesitate to seek medical attention if can't control your breathing.

The LORD is my shepherd, I shall not be in want.
He makes me lie down in green pastures, he leads
me beside quiet waters, he restores my soul. He
guides me in paths of righteousness for his names
sake. Even though I walk through the valley of the shadow
of death, I will fear no evil for you are with me; your
rod and your staff they comfort me.

Psalm 23:1-4

Fears

Fears. Books are written about them, and movies are based on them. But the Bible says we don't have to live in fear. "I will fear no evil", the psalmist wrote. Isaiah 43:5 states "Do not be afraid, for I am with you." The Lord is there to listen to your fears and to comfort you. He is concerned about you because he made you in his likeness. He made green pastures for you to lie down on. You can always turn to God if no one is present with you to talk to; talking does help.

I have extreme fears of being trapped and being killed. A large number of persons with anxiety also have co-morbid or co-occurring substance abuse issues which I will talk about later.

I am alone a lot which means that I turn to God a lot. I also don't leave my house a lot because of those fears; so since early mornings are best for me, I go the store or post office in the morning. Some people can't leave their house at all, and the next exercise addresses that. Remember, nothing worth having comes easy, so this exercise may take you months to accomplish.

1. If you have a back door, go outside and walk around the yard and just notice the grass, flowers, rocks; whatever is in your backyard. All of that was made for your enjoyment.
2. Sit and breathe in the freshness of outside, or walk around your yard for some added exercise.
3. If you are unable to go outside, try unlocking the door and leaving it that way for an hour. The next time open your back door a crack and leave it. Each day try to open it further and maybe stand in the door way looking at all there is to see in your yard.
4. Get out into the yard and walk. It is good exercise, and it increases the release of endorphins and adrenalin which makes us feel better.

I lie down and sleep; I wake again,

*because the L*ORD *sustains me.*

Psalm 3:5

Nightmares

This scripture says it all you lie down to sleep and wake again. You may awaken during the night with nightmares, but the LORD sustains you. You will get up and he will help you face another day.

I have difficulty sleeping due to anxiety and nightmares. I have learned some tips to help me fall asleep, and I have a plan if I awaken with a nightmare. To help myself fall asleep, I burn a candle or I use oils in the bedroom about two hours before I go to bed, then I blow them out before I go to bed for safety. The sense of smell is the strongest sense; by lying down and breathing deeply the scent will help calm you.

I also use this time to meditate. I close my eyes and relax my body in the bed, as best as I can. In other words I make myself as comfortable as possible. As negative thoughts come into my mind, I imagine a cloud slowly moving it away. Sometimes I have to do this several times to come to stillness. I concentrate on my breathing until it is regular and soft, then I focus on the stillness. This takes practice.

For nightmares, I have a plan. I say aloud. "This is a dream," then try to go back to sleep using meditation. If that doesn't work I get up, turn on the kitchen light, and make a cup of hot tea. The warmth makes me sleepy, and the light eases my anxiety.

Make a plan for yourself in case you have nightmares so that you will know what your routine will be. This makes it easier to return to sleep. You also want to write about the nightmare in a journal and then share the experience with the person you have chosen to be your confidant.

Imagery rehearsal also is effective in dealing with nightmares and sleep disorders. Write down your nightmare and reform it; practice the new, reformed nightmare in your head. Your therapist can go over this technique with you, as it takes several weeks and steps.

To help you fall asleep, you can try Melatonin which is a natural sleep aid found in health stores. In addition avoid drinking caffeine past 3PM, and eat early between 5 and 6PM.

Try the following relaxation exercise to help you go to sleep;

1. Lie on your bed in a comfortable position with your hands about a foot from your sides. Feel the bed supporting your entire body. Hold each position for about thirty seconds, then relax.
2. Squeeze your eye lids shut, hold, then open them wide.
3. Purse your lips together, then open your mouth wide.
4. Pull your shoulders up to your ears, then pull them away from your ears.
5. Clinch your fists, then spread your fingers wide.
6. Pull in your abdomen, then push it up. Next tilt your pelvis forward then, tilt it back into the bed.
7. Tighten you thighs and calves and release. End by bending your toes into your foot, then spreading your toes wide and relax.
8. Seek medical attention if you are unable to fall or stay asleep.

The LORD is a refuge for the oppressed,

a stronghold in times of trouble.

Psalm 9:9

External Safe Place

I seek something to hold onto in a time of trouble. It is a relief to know that God is my stronghold and I can turn to him for anything without worrying what I might say, do, or think. You are never alone even though you may feel lonely or alone during high anxiety times. God meets us where we are at and never leaves our sides, his arms cradles us. Romans 3:23-24 says, "For all have sinned and fall short of the glory of God, and are justified freely by his grace through the redemption that came by Christ Jesus." Freely we are saved through God's grace and are welcomed to him.

To help alleviate my anxiety I have an external safe place. I set up a corner in my house that has "God things", a candle, as he is my light, rosaries (my grandfather was catholic), a prayer box where I place pieces of paper I have written special prayer requests, a crucifix, the Bible, and coins of saints. I go to this place when I am having trouble and I hold onto a rock from the Euphrates River, a coin or a rosary and pray with all my heart.

The trouble with anxiety is that it manifests itself in so many symptoms, shakiness, nausea, muscle tension, flashbacks, panic attacks, accelerated heart rate, pain in the chest, headaches, sweating, avoidance, fear and more. The important thing is to have a safe place in your house where you can go when anxiety sets in. Set it up with what makes you happy and calm and use it. You may have family pictures, scenery pictures, or a favorite book.

1. Set up a corner or a room with things, and pictures that bring you joy.
2. Have a portable CD player in your safe place to listen to guided imagery (a tape or book that uses imagery to guide you in relaxation), relaxation CD's, or music that soothes you.
3. Include something of yours that is sacred to you and hold it or rub it, carry it around with you when you are having a bad time. You are grounding yourself in the present by focusing on what is in your hand instead of on your anxiety.
4. Let your family know where your safe place is and to let you be until you are ready to leave it.

The LORD is my rock, my fortress and

my deliverer, my God is my rock, in whom

I take refuge. He is my shield and the horn

of my salvation, my stronghold. I call to the

LORD, who is worthy of praise, and I am saved

from my enemies.

Psalm 18:2-3

Accepting Yourself

I like this scripture because it reminds me that I was saved from my enemies. I am alive. That doesn't mean that I am the same person as I was before. I have changed and now am living with PTSD and Depression.

Fears or events may have changed you also, but you are still a child of God that he saved from enemies. God gave us all free will and some use it for good and others for bad. But if we have life, we can learn and use skills to thrive in this new life.

One of my symptoms is hyper vigilance; meaning that I may feel fear and threats when none exist. I am overly aware of my surroundings, and my body is in a fight, flight or freeze mode. This causes difficulties on outings and muscle tension. My life now is focused on living life to its fullest with my anxieties. In the beginning of my depression and PTSD I would say I just wanted to be me again, but now I realize I am me with changes due to life experiences.

I really came to appreciate my husband because he lives with this, too, through me. He had to have been given to me by God because he never falters like I do.

You too may struggle with hyper-vigilance. The Lord is your stronghold and he will deliver you. Be aware of your environment looking around at the normalcy and repeating "I am safe". Do what you can to help others and let others help you. Ask someone to go with you and become comfortable having the nearness of your confidant. Take time to breathe, do not be in a hurry and pace yourself. Accept yourself as a whole, complete person deserving of happiness. The less stress you have the better it is for your anxiety disorder.

You family may want you back to who you were. Help them understand the new you. Give them books to read about what to expect about your specific disorder or have them learn from the Internet, as it is a great resource. I recommend families be included in the treatment process. If your anxiety stemmed from childhood, you may gain a better understanding of why you are the way you are.

Praise the Lord for the good times and fill those times with what makes you happy. Make the most of your gift of life, even though it is different now.

How priceless is your unfailing love!

Both high and low among men find

refuge in the shadow of your wings.

Psalm 36:7

Depression

Life is priceless. You can't replace it, you can't trade it in, and you can't get another one. The same is said about the unfailing love of Christ: it can't be replaced; it is and will be forever more. From the moment of your conception you were under God's wings. He said, he knew you before you were born (Jer. 1:5). It is a blessing to know that God's love does not fail and whatever our condition we are made in his image.

I sometimes think I am not enough because of my anxiety disorder. I mentioned before that I spend a great deal of time alone, which isn't good for the mind, so I have to have a good routine to keep me from the depths of depression. The thoughts we tell ourselves say a lot about our condition and where we are with it. If the thoughts are constantly negative and focused on "cannots," that doesn't leave room for the "cans".

Depression is a common co-morbid condition. It takes away our desire to do anything including taking care and nurturing ourselves. Depression can also keep you from talking to other people. To cope with my depression, I use a routine to make sure that all that I can do I am doing. Buy some easy meals for the bad days, lay out clothes for the next day the night before, talk to someone every day, and follow complete rules of hygiene.

These tips will help you cope with the bad days:

1. Make yourself a routine if you do not already have one.
2. Try to eat regularly and include foods that offer good nutrition. Do not snack often in front of the television.
3. Add a hygiene routine. Wash your face twice a day and get dressed.
4. Exercise regularly, even if it is only walking around your backyard, or doing gardening or household chores.
5. Do something you enjoy and that makes you feel good. Use all your "cans" each day.
6. If you have excessive worries or fears, write out your nighttime routine and take it around with you to make sure you haven't missed anything. This way you won't go to bed wondering if you forgot to lock the doors.

If you have uncontrolled depression and are not in counseling or do not have a psychiatrist, make today the day you schedule an appointment to see a professional who can help you.

For great is your love toward me;

you have delivered me from the

depths of the grave.

Psalm 86:13

Suicidal Ideations

Read this scripture as often as needed. You have been delivered from the depths of the grave because you were loved. In the Bible it states "there is a time for everything on earth, including a time to die" (Eccles 3:2). This is already set and figured into the equation. The fact that you are living right now proves the love God has for you and that your life is not complete. Each of us is responsible to fulfill our purpose here on earth, even though we may not know what that purpose is

I have struggled at times with suicide ideations. Once it was due to medication, but mostly is has been due to depression. During those times I talked with my psychiatrist and my husband. They both knew what was going on.

If you are have suicide ideations, seek psychiatric help now. There is a better way to live than thinking of dying. Family and friends love you and can be a support if you talk with them. You have your relationship with God to support you. Then there is just you and all that you contribute to this world just by being a part of it. I understand that anxiety can make death feel preferable, but suicide is not an answer. It is a permanent event affecting those you love. Remember that Jesus gave his life so that you can live yours.

If you utilize your confidant in a time of crisis, inform that person ahead of time not to use clichés' during those moments. You do not need to hear "It will be better tomorrow," "just don't think about it," or "it's not that bad". Have your confidant ask you open-ended questions that start you talking about your feelings; "How are you coping?" "What plan(s) do you have?" "Are you thinking of hurting yourself, how?"

In every situation there is hope. In Jeremiah 29:11 it says, "For I know the plans I have for you, declares the LORD, plans to prosper you, and not harm you, plans to give you hope and a future." Whatever your emotional pain God is always there for you.

Suicide ideations are serious. Have the number of your counselor or psychiatrist close, or call 911. There are crisis hotlines staffed by people who are trained to counsel those who need to talk to someone. The United States suicide and crisis hotlines are 1-800-SUICIDE (784-2433) or 1-800-273-TALK (8255).

For he guards the course of the just

and protects the way of his faithful ones.

Proverbs 2:8

Relationships

God guards us and wants nothing in return except to follow his word and to love him. When you think about it, he is not asking much. First, we must know the word so we can obey it, and we will love the Lord if we follow the word. He offers us his protection regardless of our sins if we have asked for his forgiveness. Our job is to follow his word. The Bible teaches about relationships with families, neighbors, spouses even enemies.

Relationships are often damaged by persons with anxiety disorders. They often shut out others from fear of rejection, being "looked at" differently, or being left alone. How many times when you have been asked, "How do you feel," you reply "fine," when that is not the truth? When you are asked that question, it is a great opportunity to really tell that person, so that he or she can understand and help. Let the person know what is helpful and what is not. Allow your family and friends to be a positive part of your struggle your anxiety.

I have been guilty of using the "fine" answer and it caused difficulties with my daughter. I was not comfortable giving my correct address and my daughter felt it was necessary. She was unaware of my fear responses. My confidant (husband) had to talk with her to help her understand.

I also catch myself using the "Fine" response with my husband sometimes, because nine times out of ten when he asks I am not fine, but I get fearful he will tire of hearing it. But that fear is in my fearful mind, not in his, and I fail to give him the opportunity to help me. Below are steps to help your family and friends to understand what helps you when your anxiety is high.

1. Write a letter to each family member letting them know what helps you when you are having an anxiety attack – for example, being by yourself for awhile to meditate.
2. Use mindfulness "an awareness that is sensitive, open, kind, gentle and curious. It arises from paying attention on purpose in a way that is nonjudging, friendly and does not try to add or subtract from whatever is happening." (Brantley and Millstine), and focus on breathing.
3. Include in the letters what others do that increases your anxiety.
4. Have a talk with each family member or give them the letter.

Every word of God is flawless;

he is a shield to those who take

refuge in him.

Proverbs 30:5

Mindfulness

The word of God is flawless, but we as humans are flawed. God is a shield where we can take refuge. He doesn't mind that we have anxiety; he still loves and shields us and we can still have refuge in him even if we do only in the time of prayer or when we are thanking him after a successful trip to the grocery store.

How many times do we need refuge? For me it is constantly throughout the day and night. I have a lot I avoid, but I can't avoid the anxiety, shaking, flashbacks, back and neck pain, or panic attacks. However I have the ability to moderate them with my thoughts, mindfulness and meditation. I tell myself to drop my shoulders, unclench my hands, breathe, and soften my abdomen. I am mindful of the events occurring in my mind and I hold the image that is causing me anxiety while doing the above and eventually the relaxation takes over and I am only mindful of my breathing.

There are a number of guided imagery, or guided relaxation CD's which you can use when seeking refuge from your anxiety.

1. Sit in a comfortable position with your shoulders relaxed and hands in your lap or lie down with your arms about a foot from your body, palms up.
2. Close your eyes and imagine a light surrounding you. Feel its warmth. Focus on the warmth of the light covering your body.
3. Push all other images and thoughts aside while you focus on the light warming your entire body.
4. Slowly include your support system in your light by watching them join you in your mind and feel their support.
5. Sit or lay there for as long as you want.

Do not be anxious about anything,

but in everything by prayer and

petition, with thanksgiving, present

your requests to God.

Philippians 4:6

Avoidance

God knew in advance that his people would have anxieties, so he set a plan for them – we present them to him. We pray about what we need to control our anxiety, and then with thanksgiving present the anxiety to him. Relieve yourself of carrying the burden alone and share it with God. Isaiah 41:10 says, "So do not fear, for I am with you; do not be dismayed for I am your God. I will strengthen you and help you; I will uphold you with my righteous right hand."

Isolation is common as we avoid people, places, events, and things that remind us of or increase our anxiety. However, isolation is not healthy, nor does it help our anxiety even though we might get temporary relief from it.

If I could, I would avoid Wal-mart, but I need my medications and food. So I have a plan for Wal-mart trips. First, I park by the closest shopping cart return bin. I know I am going to be anxious, so when I come out, I don't want to have to look for my vehicle. Second, I don't pick up my medication and groceries on the same day since they are in different locations in the store. This shortens my stay in Wal-mart. Third, I never buy more than twenty items at a time so I can go through the express lanes, which also shorten my stay. Fourth, I start in the back of the store (where there is not an exit) and work my way to the front. My anxiety decreases the closer I get to the door. Once I get in my car, I breathe for a few minutes before starting the car.

What do you avoid? Can you craft a plan to shorten your visit or lessen your anxiety? Think about the places where you get anxious, and go through an outing to those places from beginning to end. In what way can you shorten your exposure? The goal, of course, is to be able to go without anxiety, but that evolves over time.

Make a plan for your outing that covers the time you leave your house until you return. Concentrated breathing is good for these outings; to utilize on outings, breathe comfortably in and out through your nose and drop your shoulders. Your plan may include having someone you trust go with you. Remember God will also walk beside you and provide you comfort.

And the peace of God, which transcends
all understanding, will guard your hearts
and your minds in Christ Jesus.

Philippians 4:7

Anxiety

I am glad someone is guarding my heart and mind. There are times I think I am losing control, but I know better because God is guarding my mind. He is ever-present, so I am never alone. Since the peace of God transcends all understanding, I do not need to understand how he will guard my mind just that he does.

When I stated above that at times I think I am losing control, it was because my responses to fearful stimuli is so far out of proportion with the actual threat. This is commonly called anxiety where our fear response is in a fight, flight, or freeze mode. The dorsal anterior cingulate cortex (part of the brain) is involved with fear learning and expression (Shin, L. and Handwerger, K.) My fear response tends to be to flee which happens to me when I hear sirens, loud noises, or see a police vehicle.

Research in the neuroscience; field that shows positive changes in the brain called neuroplasticity by those using meditation. By being present in the now that is ever changing and allowing those changes to take place and just being with them is a part of meditation.

Meditation in the past has been called training for the heart and mind. Love, peace, joy and compassion are our exercise in meditation.

1. Sit in a comfortable position with your shoulders dropped and hands in your lap. Close your eyes and focus on what you are thinking and feeling.
2. What surrounds you; think around yourself; the walls, house, the yard, the air, sun, moon, stars including up to the whole universe.
3. Keep an open and curious mind.
4. Think of the word love. What does that conjure up in thoughts and feelings and how does it relate to or encompass the world?
5. Think of peace. What thoughts and feelings come up and how does that relate to the world?
6. Think of joy. What thoughts feelings and surrounding events does that bring up?
7. Spend some time on the word compassion. What are your thoughts and feelings? Can you feel compassion inside yourself and outside in the world?

...whatever is true, whatever is noble,

whatever is right, whatever is pure,

whatever is lovely, whatever is admirable-

if anything is excellent or praiseworthy-

think about such things.

Philippians 4:8

Meditation

Meditate/meditation is mentioned eighteen times in the Bible, so it is not a new concept. Meditation is used commonly in the Eastern World and is now quite popular in the Western World. Meditation has been researched for mental and physical disabilities with good results. Meditation is an active practice that involves sensitive attention. It is a nonjudging awareness and offers the possibility of deep understanding of self.

The psalms talk about meditation; For instance, Psalm 19:14 says "May the words of my mouth and the meditation of my heart be pleasing in your sight, O LORD, my Rock and my Redeemer". How much time do we focus on our anxiety symptoms? I experience shakiness during meals I prefer to eat alone because I drop food off my utensils which is embarrassing. I can eat with my husband and he acts like he doesn't notice which helps me be comfortable eating, but what if I have company or we are asked out to eat? I have learned to order finger foods at restaurants if I am with others. Finger foods are easier to handle which reduces my anxiety about eating with others. In turn it reduces my isolation. I also meditate in the restaurant to come to a peaceful place.

It takes great effort and determination on my part to focus on something other than my anxiety. I do meditate twice a day, gives me a reprieve. I have a mental safe place I use, along with breathing. But it did take practice for me in order to meditate without focusing on anxiety, so do not give up. Be persistent in your efforts.

1. Sit or lie in a comfortable position, close your eyes and concentrate on what is admirable about yourself. Stay with that for about five minutes.
2. Now think about your family and what is admirable about them.
3. Now focus on what is admirable about the world.
4. Think about God and what is admirable and praiseworthy about him. Stay with that as long as you can.
5. Sit quietly and feel what comes to mind. If it is negative, let it drift by like clouds. Just listen with your heart and feel what your mind brings up.

6. When you are ready, rise up and write down some admirable, noble, pure or lovely things that came up and tape it to your bathroom mirror where you can read it every day.

I have learned the secret of being content

in any and every situation, whether well fed or hungry,

whether living in plenty or want. I can do

everything through him who gives me strength.

Philippians 4:12-13

Isolation

What hard words to carry out!   Being content in your situation includes more than just getting through a day. You have to accept your limitations and situation and be satisfied in how you are living. By leaning on God you have a strong ally who will help you along the way.   In Romans it goes farther than learning to be content it says, "But we also rejoice in our sufferings, because we know that suffering produces perseverance, perseverance character; and character hope. And hope does not disappoint us, because God has poured out his love into our hearts". Romans 5:3-5.

I spent too much time being upset at myself, my situation, and my anxiety symptoms. I didn't call or talk with anyone in any real terms because, I was so depressed. Thankfully, my husband, daughter and parents routinely called. I was so focused on all that was lost and upset that I didn't have control of myself let alone my life. I was so consumed by my disorder that I couldn't focus on much of anything else. Just getting up and paying bills was all I could muster for the day.   However I was continually on the move around the house. I couldn't sit still. I couldn't rest. It was as if I was trying to run from my symptoms, but they were always there.

This exercise helped for me be content with the changes in myself and my isolation.

1. Sit or lie comfortably and repeat, "I completely love and accept myself, even though I have anxiety."
2. Now say aloud "I accept myself and my anxiety as the whole me in God, complete and content."
3. Repeat the steps ten times. Use it throughout the day each time you start negative thinking.

"Therefore do not worry about tomorrow,
for tomorrow will worry about itself. Each
day has enough trouble of its own"

Matthew 6:34

Excessive Worries

I used to worry about everything. When will I have another panic attack? What if someone broke in? Are the doors locked? What if this lasts forever. What if I never can return to work What about finances? What if I am stopped by the police? Did I take my medicine? What if my husband tires of my condition?

Some of these worries were relieved by simple strategies. For example a friend bought me a medication container that I filled with my medications for morning, noon and night. Then if I questioned if I took my medicine, I could just check the container. At work, I had to resign that I could not work like I used to, but I could still be of benefit in my field. For these and each of my other worries I have learned that I don't have to worry about tomorrow it will come with its own set of worries when I wake up, so I just focus on one day at a time.

You too can learn to focus on one day at a time. These steps will help you do that:

1. Each evening make a list of what you have to do tomorrow. Include taking medications, hygiene, meditation and prayer.
2. List what you would like to accomplish. This part of the list is flexible and can be rescheduled based on your day.
3. Be realistic and keep your mind flexible.
4. At the end of the day make a new list. You may have to carry some items over. Or you may have accomplished everything on your list and you can see what you can really do.

"Ask and it will be given to you; seek and you will find; knock and the door will be opened to you. For everyone who asks receives; he who seeks finds; and to him who knocks, the door will be opened".

Matthew 7:7-8

Be Active in Your Treatment

This verse is active; it takes an effort on your part, but it tells you what will happen. Continue to pray for what you want knowing that God will provide what is best for you. Be real about yourself, as the Bible states your (God's) will be done (Matt 7:10). And in Isaiah it says, "so will your God rejoice over you" (Isa. 62:5).

In the beginning I listened to my counselors, psychiatrists and family without asking questions or challenging them about knowing my life and capabilities and without doing my own research or relying on my own knowledge. You can guess my progress did not go well. It wasn't until I began researching, questioning, and informing my helping professionals what was and was not working in my life that changes occurred.

For example, my psychiatrist was not aware that Yoga had been receiving good reviews in studies as a treatment for my symptoms. I began practicing Yoga, and I feel relaxed while I am doing it and better throughout the day. It is a time my mind is free of anxiety and stillness is present in the moves.

Likewise, the professionals you are seeing can have a complete picture only with information you provide to them. They need your help to help you. If you have delayed in getting treatment and your life is not where you can control your anxieties, now is the time to ask and seek treatment. If you are maintaining well on your own, it would still be useful to seek more information and treatment interventions which may improve your quality of life.

Be active in your treatment, whether you see a professional or you do the research on your own. Try some new interventions, whether you find them in this book or through your own research.

But the fruit of the Spirit is love, joy,

peace, patience, kindness, ... and self-control

Galatians 6:22-23

The Spirit

The Spirit is available to you through your acceptance of Christ. The Bible was written by the inspiration/Spirit of the Lord. The Spirit is all around us and in us. He is the embodiment of love; let us move toward that love. It is the embodiment of joy; let us feel joy by pushing out the fears. Let us experience moments of peace when we feel safe. Let us practice patience with our-selves and those we love. Let us be kind and forgiving of ourselves and thereby gain some control over the fears that hound us.

Joy, peace, patience, kindness and self-control often are lacking in those with an anxiety disorder. They've lost the ability to feel joy, their peace is interrupted by their fears, they don't demonstrate patience (calmly), they usually are not kind to themselves they lack self-control.

The Spirit gives us all these. Whom do you love? Love the Lord God with all your heart and mind. Have you let others into your world? What brought you joy before? Is it something that you can still do, or do you need to find a new avenue for your joy? Where do you find peace? How do you develop patience? How do you demonstrate kindness to yourself and others? How do you practice self-control?

God gives me love and I love him. I also have my family and friends because I have let them into my world and they are not frightened when I have a flashback, panic attack, or react to something I find fearful. Yoga gives me joy, peace and patience. I also find joy in my family, the grass growing, the sun shining, and the Bible. Kindness toward myself is hard and I have to work at it as I am usually judging myself and looking at what I lack versus what I have. Self-control I find in knowledge, Yoga, meditation, positive self-talk and grounding (being aware of what is around you. For example, couch, pillows, pictures – things that connect you to the Here and Now).

The exercise below is to provide self-awareness and comfort of a support system.

1. Write down all those you love.
2. Write down what gives you joy and peace and; how you use patience and self-control.

3. Think of yourself you are right now, you are loveable and deserving of joy and peace.
4. Who will stand with you in the depths of your anxiety and not run in fear? You have God. Can you bring another into your fold who understands you because you have educated that person?

"Who of you by worrying can add a single hour to his life? Since you cannot do this very little thing, why do you worry about the rest?

Luke 12:25-26

Social Phobia

What an awesome and powerful God we have, calling a single hour of life a little thing. All things are possible through him. He cares that we have worries but lets us know we cannot improve our situation by worrying.

Give your worries up to the Lord, do what you can, and be satisfied for that moment. Live each day as a practice for life. Add things you can, accept things you cannot control, and use your resources to the fullest.

First Corinthians 2:9 says "No eye has seen, no ear has heard, no mind has conceived what God has prepared for those who love him – but God has revealed it to us by his Spirit". No one knows what is in store for us, but we can count on it being magnificent.

At a meeting, I was up for an award. I was petrified that I would win because I would have to give a speech in front of all my peers. When my name was called, I was so anxious that I was shaking. I took a moment and thought. *God is with me and I cannot die by giving a speech.* Because I get anxious around a lot of people I was petrified to walk up on stage. I sucked in my breath and thought, *I cannot do this*, as I took a deep breath and walked to the podium. I do not remember what I said, and I know my speech was fast. But the important thing is that I stopped worrying about it and did it. God restored my strength enough for me to accomplish a task that should have been exciting but for me was wrought with worry.

If you cannot add a single hour to your life, then why worry about everything else.

1. Take one worry that you have and pray on it; focus and meditate, see what comes to your mind.
2. If needed talk it over with your confidant, counselor or anyone else you choose. You may discover that what you were worrying about had a simpler answer then you thought.
3. Or, that the solution to the problem needs to be broken down into smaller steps to be accomplished.

In an anxious state, we do not always concentrate effectively which is why a trusted outside opinion may be needed.

Cast all your anxiety on him

because he cares for you.

1 Peter 5:7

Anxieties

What an easy task this sounds, but how difficult this is to accomplish. God is calling for you to give him all your anxieties and he will take care of them and you will be free. God states this because he cares for you and wants you to have him in your life. Jeremiah 31:4 states "I will build you up again and you will be rebuilt…and go out and dance with the joyful". We are not only asked to give up our anxieties but to be joyful.

My anxiety was so embedded in fears that I had difficulty to just let God have it. I pray everyday that he is with me as I tackle tasks. It may be to let me have a safe trip, attend a volunteer meeting without a panic attack, cook a meal for my husband, talk with at least one person, to not suffer in pain from tension, or to let me get through the day without a flashback.

As you noticed above I break down my anxieties and asked for relief for just each part. This has been successful for me. It is easier to work on parts of your anxiety rather than to focus on all the dimensions at once. It is overwhelming to focus on all parts of your anxiety, and that keeps you stagnant in your progress. Allowing yourself to focus on one thing at a time and meditate will help you live a full life with your anxiety. As one symptom comes into alignment with your life, you can then focus on another aspect and over time all aspects are aligned in your life.

This exercise focuses on God's love and the comfort he provides.

1. Sit or lie comfortably, shoulders away from the ears.
2. Focus on God's love for you. Let it come inside you. Feel it move with your breath in and out.
3. If anxious thoughts come up, acknowledge them and let them go.
4. Continue focusing on God's love; let it fill you.
5. Feel the support you are getting from the ground and chair. Relax in it. Stay there as long as you want.

"I have come into the world as a light,

so that no one who believes in me

should stay in darkness".

John 12:46

Your Social Being

God is light, and he shares that light with us so that we can feel safe and secure. He states that no one who believes in him will stay in darkness. At night he even gives us a moon and billions of stars so that we can have hope of his light shining through.

Isolation leads to darkness, you are cut off from everything and everyone. You are alone with only your thoughts to keep you company, and most often this leads to negative thinking and an   unsatisfied life. We are made to be social beings, to interact with others and be a part of a group or family. In your fears the light is not shining through, nor are you allowing God's light to come in. If you continually shut out people, they eventually give up trying to get in. So it is up to you to be proactive and have at least one confidant whom you regularly communicate with, sharing your thoughts, no matter how dark, so that person can help you.

I have to work on not isolating myself and I am not the best person on reaching out. But I have told my husband all that I am going through, so he understands. Some other family members and friends know a lot and will listen to me when I call. It is frightening at night to have a nightmare, flashback, fears, or panic attacks, so have at least one person you can call at night too.

It is also common for some with anxiety disorders to use alcohol or non prescription pills to mask the symptoms, but this adds another layer of darkness to your disorder. The symptoms still exist, and you are not using self-monitoring, self-control or skills you have learned to manage those symptoms.

To prevent isolation, try some tips below.

1. Use your plan for night time, call or talk to your confidant at times of crisis.
2. Turn to your spiritual self when needed.
3. Invite someone over for coffee or meet them at a coffee shop.
4. Go to a restaurant with your confidant.

May the God of hope fill you with all joy and peace as you trust in him, so that you may overflow with hope by the power of the Holy Spirit.

Romans 15:13

Hopelessness

Do not give up hope that your condition will improve and that you will be able to live a comfortable life without the anxiety controlling your life. This is not a short process and it takes patience, endurance, and trust. But if you rely on God your work towards your new life will be easier to attain. You will overflow with hope, and he will never leave your side. He is there when you call and will listen to you always.

Hopelessness is an empty feeling; it gives nothing back but absorbs all. It does not help but hinders your successes. It is also hard to get away from. Hopelessness is a heavy weight to bear and will drag you down with it. Its company is loneliness and it enjoys that company and works on you not to break their bond.

One way to avoid hopelessness is by having a confidant and using that person. Another way is by will power, to use your skills and God's help in living your life instead of giving up. The Bible says, "if hope deferred makes the heart sick" (Proverbs 13:12). Listen to your heart and hear the cries for hope in your life.

1. Sit or lie in a comfortable position, shoulders away from the ears.
2. Repeat this statement "I am worthy of living. I am loveable. I am meaningful to those who love me".
3. Now say aloud, "I accept my whole self and find I am a piece of art formed by God".
4. After about fifteen minutes, get up and do something. It can be chores, making a phone call, sitting in your back yard, reading, taking a hot bath, or burning a scented candle and just breathing in the fragrance.

"In your anger do not sin": Do not let
the sun go down while you are still angry.

Ephesians 4:26

Anger

Anger is a natural emotion and probably one of the most recognized physically, by body language and voice inflicion by others. God gives two instructions in regards to anger; do not sin, and do not let the sun go down while you are still angry. These may sound impossible for you to carry out, but with God on your side you can accomplish both of these.

It may take a lot of prayer to control your anger. Your anxiety may contribute to something that was done to you or something you witnessed; by coming out as anger. Your anger may be turned inward which is depression. No matter how you became angry, you need to release it as it is a stumbling block to your optimal health. Forgiveness is the best way to get rid of the anger. This does not mean that you forget or that the one or ones that wronged you will be close to you, but at least on your part they have been forgiven.

Practice thinking before you act. You do not want to say or do something that you later regret.   When you become angry, walk away, listen to music, and breathe calmly. Try the Gestalt Empty Chair technique (Corey, G.):

1. Sit in a chair facing another chair.
2. Pretend that the offending person/persons are sitting in the empty chair.
3. Tell them why you are angry, what they did that upset you.
4. Tell them you were and are a loveable person.
5. Carry on this conversation until you have said all you want the other person(s) to hear.
6. Get up from your chair.   You should feel some weight lifted from your shoulders.

The good thing about forgiveness is that you do not have to face the ones you are forgiving. You can do it in speech to an empty chair, in prayer, or in writing a letter you don't mail.

If you think you may not be able to handle the emotions that may come up, complete this exercise in your counselor's office.

Oh, my anguish, my anguish!

I writhe in pain.

Jeremiah 4:19

Pain

Jeremiah expressed his anguish about the forthcoming destruction to his land by crying out to God. God responded by telling Jeremiah to go into the city, and if he found one person who dealt honestly and sought the truth, God would forgive the city. This is yet another example from scripture that God is a forgiving God.

Persons with anxiety are in pain mentally and sometimes physically and may not get the appropriate care. I mentioned in the foreword that I recommend a complete physical because the physical pain that is sometimes associated with anxiety may feel like a heart attack, gastrointestinal problems. Some of the physical symptoms of anxiety include nausea, upset stomach, neck or back pain, headaches, chest pain, shaking or trembling, diarrhea, or constipation.

Some treatments for these physical ailments include biofeedback, massage, acupuncture, Yoga, breathing exercises or chiropractic care. I have tried all five, and the least effective for me was the acupuncture.

It is amazing the tension we carry constantly in our bodies. As mentioned the body keeps score. You may find that pain enters a specific location on you. Treat that location kindly. I use Yoga daily to stretch the muscles to reduce the pain – and keep my mind off my anxiety. Breathing at a slow pace in and out through your nose is effective at reducing pain.

Try this stretch to loosen your muscles.

1. Place your feet wide apart and keep all four corners of your feet on the ground. Feel your feet connected to the ground.
2. Bend forward from the hip and place your hands on your shins, ankles, or the floor in line with your feet.
3. Let your spine and neck hang. Do not lock your knees.
4. Gently shake your head side to side. Turning the body upside down helps rejuvenate the brain.
5. Do this for about a minute then slowly rise back up to a standing position.

If this pose causes you any pain, do not complete it unless your doctor says it's okay. You should feel a stretch in your legs, spine, neck, and arms.

Dear friends, do not be surprised at the
painful trial you are suffering, as though
something strange were happening to you.

1 Peter 4:12

Normalizing

The next verse in 1 Peter says to "rejoice that you participate in the sufferings of Christ, so that you may be overjoyed when his glory is revealed" (v. 13). The suffering that accompanies your anxiety is not a surprise given that between 20 and 37% of the population have an anxiety disorder. In fact, If you know someone who is suffering with an anxiety disorder, consider adding that person to your list of confidants.

There is an explanation and diagnosis to the anxiety you feel; it is normal in certain situations.

I felt no one could understand me and what I was going through. As a counselor, I met several clients with these disorders and I knew what to advise them, but now that I am living with a disorder talk therapy was not effective. I have more empathy and personal experience in treating these disorders because of my research and my own trials.

Stretching and breathing help open the chest and reduce tension in the body while strengthening the major muscles of your back in this exercise. Feeling normal often requires more exercise and release of tension.

1. Sit on the floor in a simple cross-legged position with the right foot in front, Indian style.
2. Place your hands behind you and take an in breath, raising your chest, and an out breath, relaxing.
3. Do this three times.
4. Now walk your hands forward to a comfortable position and relax your neck, letting it hang.
5. Wait about thirty seconds, then come back to sitting.
6. Repeat the sequence with the left leg in front.

He gives strength to the weary and

increases the power of the weak.

Isaiah 40:29

Weariness

Constant anxiety can cause one to be weary and weak. God offers us strength and power. He is everlasting in his endurance. He never fails to be present and never tires of listening to his people. His love is unending and his support to his people everlasting. He will lift you up on eagles' wings.

I have mentioned there are times that I can't even cook dinner. I am either too anxious to focus or too weary from being anxious. I have never been one to take naps, but I find that a couple times a week I have to have a nap to rest after an anxiety attack or because of tension. I use to think by that by taking a nap that I wasn't *doing*, but I have learned that being, whether taking a nap or meditating is more important than doing some of the time. I have learned that I do not always have to do, that sometimes I can just be, and that is enough.

You are not judged by which deeds you do but by how you are (being). God restores us. He takes our anxieties and weaknesses and gives us new strengths with a new plan for our life.

This exercise is for your body and mind and is intended to illicit relaxation and renews your strength. Try to relax your body into the support of the floor.

1. Sit or lie in a comfortable position.
2. Close your eyes and let your mind wander. As negative thoughts come to mind, just let them float by like clouds.
3. Be aware of your support from where you are sitting or lying. Notice that you do not have to exert any effort to sit or lie there.
4. Be aware of where you are physically and of your breath.
5. Let your breath travel to where you feel weak and breathe energy into that area.
6. Scan your whole body with your breath and let it energize you.

Breathing efficiently and effectively is a very powerful tool. In fact, life cannot be sustained without it. Practice your breathing techniques frequently.

(B)ut those who hope in the LORD will

renew their strength.   They will soar

on wings like eagles; they will; run and

not grow weary, they will walk and not be faint.

Isaiah 40:31

Hope

Have hope in the Lord; have hope in life. He promises to renew our strength and that we will soar, run, and walk. He doesn't state that these things will always occur, but they will occur at times so that our hope remains strong. Sometimes we have to walk instead of run, especially when we are dealing with a debilitating disorder. It takes perseverance and active participation.

Holding onto hope is holding onto life. Whatever anxieties you face today God can use to rebuild you.

I mentioned that I rarely drive and if I do it is just to the store or post office. If I have to go any distance, then my parent's take me due to my fears. I was stopped once by the police for running over a curb and was given a sobriety test due to the medications I was on. With God's help I was able to pass and was released, but the fear is still with me because that was my second run stop by the police both since I developed PTSD. So I walk and don't run, but when I complete an errand it feels as if I am soaring on eagle's wings because of my accomplishment.

When do you soar? When do you float through a period of time without fears and anxiety? Is there a place, event, or time when all is right in your world, when the stars line up and the pain is diminished and your hopes are high and you feel joyful? When it happens, hold onto that feeling and let it glide through your body. Wiggle your arms and dangle your feet, and just feel.

1. Think of a time when you were happy.
2. Where in your body can you feel it? Let the feeling spread throughout your body.
3. Who else was present and what were they doing?
4. Focus on the feeling of happiness. Let happy thoughts in and expand to happy events in your city, state, and the world.
5. Just enjoy the feeling. Don't do anything.

No one whose hope is in you will ever

be put to shame. Show me your ways,

O LORD, teach me your paths; guide me

in your truth and teach me, for you are

God my Savior and my hope is in you all day

long. Remember, O LORD, your great mercy and love ...

Psalm 25:3-6

Patience

The word of God is the way and the path, and you will never go astray if you follow it. Focus on "my hope is in you all day long" in the versus above. How much time do you devote to God - reading the Bible, attending services, for instance and do you do these things with a joyful heart?

The time I spend with God is usually free of anxiety, but I have to focus. I walk around the house breathing in and saying, "God" and breathing out saying, "loves" and "I feel good". I also use Christian music to lift me up and spa music to relax and calm me. It took patience just hear the music without disrupting thoughts.

I mentioned before I used to think God left me; otherwise I wouldn't be witnessing and experiencing these terrible events. It was a dark time for me without God's light. It wasn't until I turned back to God - he never turned from me - that I began to control my anxiety level. I still take medication and see a psychiatrist and a chiropractor, but I am stabilized if I stick with my plan. And since I know myself better than anyone else, it was up to me to make the plan, set the outings and, appointments. and schedule my activities for my comfort level. You, too, will have to make a plan for your comfort level. Try to push the limits little by little, be patient and take your time.

Be patient with your body too. Twisting motions help relax muscles and aides in digestion.

1. Sit in a crossed-leg position with the right foot in front, Indian style.
2. Place both hands on your knees. Take a deep breath, filling your chest.
3. Let your breath out and twist to the left with your right hand on your left knee and left hand behind you.
4. Sit straight on your pubic bones. Hold for about thirty seconds then, turn back to the center.
5. Twist to the right with your left hand on your right knee. Hold for about thirty seconds then, turn back to the center.
6. Place the left foot in front and repeat the sequence to the left, then to the right.

There is surely a future hope for you,
and your hope will not be cut off.

Proverbs 23:18

Dreams

Your hope will not be cut off; God will continue to hold out hope for you even when you give up hope. We have talked about hopelessness and how that is thrives in darkness, not the light. The light of God gives hope for all who believe. God wants us to live in the light and provides a whole book as a guidance that is full of love and hope. You may not be where you want to be yet; keep hoping, praying, and being proactive in your treatment. Romans 12:12-13 encourages "Be joyful in hope, patient in affliction, faithful in prayer." Share with God's people who are in need. Practice hospitality."

I am not yet where I know I can be. I want to drive for distances without fears. I want to hear sounds and not retreat into flashbacks. I want to not have pain from the tension, and I want to be a better wife and mother. So I am still a work in progress, but I have God on my side and the Spirit in my heart, and each day I feel more content in my new life. Before I wouldn't walk out of my house; now I spend most mornings in my backyard with my coffee. I volunteer to help others, which is one of my dreams.

Think back to when you were first diagnosed and gradually review the steps that you have taken to control your anxiety. You didn't make progress overnight; that has been a gradual process. Your life will continue to change as you work on living with anxiety until you come to a point where you are content. If you are stuck in a certain spot, be patient and continue to work on that aspect.

What do you hope for? What do you dream? Dreams open up a whole new world for us, one that is good and refreshing. Dreaming is different than wishing. You might wish to win the lottery, but a dream is an ache inside you, a yearning, something you would love to do.

Dreaming opens up our creative side.

1. What can you create?
2. Can you draw, paint, do woodwork, arrange flowers, etc?
3. Follow your dreams; make them realistic.
4. Think of something you can do then complete it.

Return to your fortress, O prisoners of
hope; even now I announce that I will
restore twice as much to you.

Zechariah 9:12

A Mental Safe Place

"Return to your fortress": God instructs the prisoners of hope. He promises to restore twice as much to them and free the prisoners. You, too, can be freed by the hand of God, which reaches everywhere. Your fortress may be in God. If so he is already with you as you are and where you are. He will never leave you.

When we find ourselves trapped by situations that have no end in sight, we need to draw on the courage and power of the LORD Jesus Christ. Sometimes anxiety can feel like a prison. Our movements are set by our symptoms, and they control us. But God is telling us to return to our fortress, a safe place that is free of fears and full of peace. Where is your fortress? In a previous devotional we made a safe place in your home. Now it's time to develop a mental safe place. Use this when you cannot go physically to your safe place in your house, maybe when you are away from home, perhaps your counselor's office, you may become fearful due to a conversation.

I used to love to fly, I didn't care where I was going, I just wanted to fly. After my trauma I was fearful of flying because I was trapped inside the plane and couldn't get out. Part of my trauma was being captured, so being able to get away quickly was important. I couldn't even get a Pap smear because I was afraid of being undressed and unable to run. I had a suitcase packed with some clothes and important documents and my purse and keys ready by the garage door. That was my escape route.

To overcome my fear of flying I visualized a safe place, (my safe place is on the atolls of Maldive Islands with my husband). I also had a friend travel with me, and got an aisle seat so I could at least get up and walk and use breathing exercises. First I made a short flight, then another longer one accompanied by my friend, and then I made a solo flight. Now I enjoy flying again using my coping skills.

Setting up your mental safe place.

1. Visualize a place where you feel safe. Describe it using all your senses.
2. What do you see?
3. What do you hear?

4. What do you touch or what touches you? It could be the wind.
5. What do you smell?
6. What do you taste?
7. Make it detailed, then give it a name. Or you can just use "safe place."
8. When your anxiety level gets too high, say the name and you should begin conjuring up a picture of your safe place. You may have to prompt yourself by asking about the five senses.

And now these three remain;

faith, hope and love. But the

greatest of these is love.

1 Corinthians 13:13

Faith, Hope, and Love

Faith it is multifaceted, faith in God, faith in life, faith in self, faith in others and faith in organization. We begin with faith in God, believing even when we don't see (Heb. 11:1) and believing in the word of God. We have to have the faith that life is worth living. It is where we have relationships and have hope for the future. It is important that we believe in ourselves, the beauty that is inside, the goodness waiting to be shared. Faith in others is important too. We may have been let down by some people, but we cannot make a judgment not to trust anyone. Many people are trustworthy and can be our mentors. As for faith in organization, the first thing that comes to mind is a church, but there are other organizations that we can have faith in and be members of.

Hope we have covered, to continue to improve our lives. Hope that we are able to live life to its fullest and be joyful in the life we have been given.

The purest love is the love of God, but we have others in our life who loves us and whom we love. Love never fails. It upholds people, churches, groups, and the world.

We are lovable beings. We are able to give and receive love, and we can love the Lord with all our hearts. We have enough room for love of family, friends, and acquaintances. Our love knows no bounds except for the ones we set.

The following exercise will help you recognize how much you are capable of loving.

1. Sit or lie comfortably.
2. Focus on your breathing in and out (through your nose).
3. On your in breath state, "I love."
4. On your out breath list something or someone. Go through a complete list of people and things you love.

To them God has chosen to make known

among the Gentiles the glorious riches of

this mystery, which is Christ in you, the hope

of glory.

Colossians 1:27

Flashbacks

We are told the mystery is Christ in us, the hope of glory. Christ died willingly on the cross for us and our sins. He became flesh and suffered for us. He made a new covenant that whoever believes in him shall have ever-lasting life. He left the New Testament for us to follow, which explains forgiveness and salvation. It also tells us how to live and love.

My daughter, Brandy, was visiting with my grandchildren when an aerosol can exploded and landed by my house (I found out what it was later). At that moment I had a flashback of bombings. I was in my bathroom and immediately fell to the floor with extreme fear. My daughter came in and sat beside me for quite a while and talked in a soothing voice. Eventually I was able to come to the present and leave my bathroom.

Sometimes part of the mystery is that God uses other people to touch our lives and comfort us. On that day God used Brandy to be with me, offering me hope.

The demonstration of God's love for us by sharing this mystery proves that we are worthy individuals of the greatest love of all. We talked before about being versus doing. With God's love, it is just our being that is worthy of the hope of glory. The U. S. Army has a slogan, "Be all you can be," and that is true here. With your anxiety, which is a part of you, be all you can be and that will be enough.

1. Sit or lie comfortably.
2. Focus on your breathing and imagine that it is love spreading through you as you inhale and exhale.
3. Repeat the phrase. "The hope of glory is in me."
4. Feel your breath through your body; begin at your head and work your way down to your toes.

But since we belong to the day,

let us be self-controlled, putting

on faith and love as a breastplate,

and the hope of salvation as a helmet.

1 Thessalonians 5:8

Supportive Relationships

God asks us to be self-controlled. Notice he says to put on faith and love as a breastplate; this covers and protects our hearts. The hope of salvation protects our minds. So we are protected even when we do not feel it. We are safe in God's loving hands. What a beautiful visualization to meditate on.

My mind wanders to bad places on a daily basis. I have to focus on leaving those places and coming back into the light. Three years ago, I injured my relationship with my daughter because of where I was in my mind and what I said to her at the time. It took communication on my part to let her know where I was and what she did that took me further into the depths of anxiety and fear. She is now a good support for me and we have what I hope is a mutually satisfying relationship.

We need relationships that are strong, moral, mutually supportive, loving, and kind. Relationships are a scale that moves up and down. Sometimes we give more and sometimes we receive more. Anxiety disorders make it difficult to maintain relationships, but it is important for our overall health. Start by building your relationship with God and expand out to family and friends.

As the example with my daughter shows communication is key to healthy relationships. We talked above about writing a letter to family members about your triggers, what you need and what they can do. In this exercise you are going to ask your family what they need from you and discuss how you can meet that or if it needs to be modified. You may need to practice this exercise first with your confidant.

1. Ask them what hurts them that you do and come to some form of agreement on what you do and how they perceive it.
2. Remember, they are not judging you they are trying to make your relationships stronger.
3. Be open and honest.
4. At this time you may not be able to change a lot, but small steps eventually lead to larger steps and to wholeness.

We have this hope as an anchor for
the soul, firm and secure. It enters the
sanctuary behind the curtain, where
Jesus who went before us, has entered
on our behalf.

Hebrews 6:19-20

Hypervigilance and Tension

Jesus has done the work for us; all we have to do is follow. He gives us a book with instructions on how to follow. He gave up his life so that we can have everlasting life, and he provided a way to gain forgiveness even when we falter. We just have to ask for forgiveness. Because of our anxiety we have been humbled. The Bible describes the benefits of humility. Psalm 37:11 says, "But the meek will inherit the land and enjoy great peace." And Matthew 5:3-5 says, "Blessed are the poor in spirit, for theirs is the kingdom of heaven. … Blessed are the meek, for they will inherit the earth."

I know that my soul is firm and secure, but I need that for my physical body too. I have hypervigilance. My body is ever ready for fight, flight, or freeze. My muscles are tense, and I have pain due to the tenseness It is hard for me to relax. That is why I use Yoga and meditation. Throughout the day I use various stretches.

You may feel tension and pain in your body. If so, the stretches I use may benefit you. The following stretch, an exercise I learned from my chiropractor to release neck tension, should not hurt. You should feel a gentle stretch. If you feel pain, you are stretching too far.

1. Keep your shoulders pulled down and bend your left ear to your left shoulder. Hold for fifteen seconds, then straighten.
2. Bend your right ear to your right shoulder. Hold for fifteen seconds, then straighten.
3. Bend your chin down to your chest. Hold for fifteen seconds, then straighten.
4. Pull your head back toward your spine. Hold for fifteen seconds, then straighten.
5. Turn your head to look over your left shoulder. Hold for fifteen seconds, then straighten.
6. Turn your head to look over your right shoulder. Hold for fifteen seconds, then straighten.

*"Be careful, or your hearts will be
weighed down with dissipation,
drunkenness and the anxieties of life,
and that day will close on you
unexpectedly like a trap. For it will
come upon all those who live on the
face of the whole earth."*

Luke 21:34-35

Substance Abuse

Jesus Christ is talking in this verse to his disciples. He is talking about the second coming of Christ and through the Holy Spirit he is telling us to be careful of these things. The burden of being weighed down by dissipation, drunkenness, and the anxieties of life interrupts relationships, including the one with God. Since God is a forgiving God, we can build our relationship with him regardless of what we have done in the past.

Dissipation is another term for disintegration which can also mean "intemperate living" such as excessive drinking. Substance abuse interferes with your daily life. You may think that you feel better when you abuse alcohol or some other drug, but you are actually stuck in the same place you were, or even regressed. In addition, you may have increased relationship problems, legal problems, and financial problems. Stopping the use of substances usually requires the help from a professional. Stopping the use of substances usually requires help from a professional. Alcohol Anonymous and /or Narcotics Anonymous are a good place to start, but I would recommend conjunctive counseling for the addictions.

Do not use alcohol or illegal substances. God provides warning signs for those abusing substances; they may come in the form of a driving violation or legal issues, family problems, isolation, or financial problems. Head these warnings and take action by reaching out for treatment and to God who will stand with you throughout your struggles.

Self-medicating is not the answer. Breaking the habit will take an active role on your part. You will have to face the feelings associated with anxiety. If you are feeling them instead of numbing them, recovery can begin. Galatians 5:13 says, "You, my brothers, were called to be free. But do not use your freedom to indulge the sinful nature; rather serve one another in love."

An anxious heart weighs a man down,

but a kind word cheers him up.

Proverbs 12:25

The Burden of Anxiety

Anxiety can be a burden in our lives that weighs us down, but we do not have to shoulder that burden alone. We have to work through the disorder, but as Jesus said in Matthew 11:28 "Come to me, all you who are weary and burdened, and I will give you rest". Further on in the scripture he states that his burden is light (v. 30). He even carries all of ours. "Praise to the Lord, to God our Savior who daily bears our burdens" (Ps. 68:19).

The second part of Proverbs talks about a kind word that cheers us up. When you are around people who are positive, understanding, and joyful, it is contagious and we smile, if only for a moment. Second Corinthians 1:3-4 states, "Praise be to the God and Father of our Lord Jesus Christ, the Father of compassion and the God of all comfort, who comforts us in all our troubles, so that we can comfort those in any trouble with the comfort we ourselves have received from God. " You yourself may prove comfort to your family or friends or a stranger whom you meet. But that takes self-care; you have to be at a comfort level to comfort others.

Rachel, a friend of mine, works as a child abuse and neglect investigator and often has to remove kids from their families or homes where they reside. She has a stressful job and an anxiety disorder. She has had to learn self-care, the ability to care for herself and treat herself in a good and positive way. She has an adjusted work schedule that was completed by her psychiatrist and American Disabilities Act (ADA) where she works a certain amount of days and then is off for a week. Talk with your psychiatrist if you think an adjusted work schedule could help you cope with your anxiety.

Rachel also suffers panic attacks that are brought on by anger and frustration. Notice that she knows her triggers. Her way of calming down, when possible is to place her head in the freezer, breathing in the cold air, or drinking ice-cold water. I use ice-cold water with angry clients a lot, drinking slows down one's breathing and the coolness enters your body.

As anxiety often leads to tension the exercise below helps by stretching the muscles in a nurturing way.

1. Lie on the floor with your arms by your side, palms up, and feet stretched out.

2. Bring your knees to your chest and hug them by wrapping your arms around the back of your thighs, shins, or knees. Notice how that straightens your back and your thoracic and lumbar vertebrae are on the floor.
3. Hold this position for about thirty seconds, then release your legs to a straight-out position. Stretch your arms over your head and rest them on the floor.
4. Repeat this for five times. On your next knee-to-chest position slightly move your body from left to right, massaging your spine. Do this for about a minute.
5. Come to a resting position with your legs down, your feet turned out, and your arms resting about a foot from your body, palms up. Rest as long as you want.

God is our refuge and strength,

an ever-present help in trouble.

Psalm 46:1

Obsessions and Compulsions

God is omnipresent and never sleeps so that we can. Psalm 4:8 says, "I will lie down and sleep in peace, for you alone, O LORD make me dwell in safety." He is always present - in our times of need and our times of joy. For each moment we live Christ lives in us until eternity. *As* Ezekiel 37:26 says, "I will make a covenant of peace with them; it will be an everlasting covenant"

I have obsessive-compulsive traits. They are most prevalent at bedtime. I can be like the Energizer Bunny at bedtime. I think, did I lock the front door? I get up just to lie down and then think about the back door. I go check and then think about the garage door. All my obsessions concern safety. During the day I run around checking the stove, coffee pot, and the ceiling fans clean (are they clean?).

I have had to practice slowing my mind and focusing on one thing. This is where meditation, Yoga and Bible study is helps. God promised us peace, and he will provide it. It's an everlasting promise, but we have to do our part. I schedule moments for meditation, Yoga and Bible study, along with prayer time. In these times I am undisturbed by the anxious thoughts.

Perhaps you can relate to racing thoughts, obsessions and the compulsions. What can you do to reduce them? Earlier we made a plan for your nighttime routine. Review your plan at this time and add any obsessions that you can routinely check so that you are not just jumping about.

This exercise will take you from thoughts of your mind to your physical self.

1. Sit on the floor in a comfortable crossed-leg position. Check your back by rubbing your lower spine to ensure you are sitting upright. You should not have any protruding discs; if you do, elevate your hips with a blanket or pillow.
2. Raise your arms above your head and interlace your fingers, turning the palms up, elbows straight.
3. Bend to the right, keeping your hips even on the floor. Hold for thirty seconds, then straighten.
4. Bend to the left, keeping your hips level on the floor. Hold for thirty seconds, then straighten.
5. Place your palms on your knees. Check your spine alignment and repeat the exercise five times.

You will not fear the terror of night,

nor the arrow that flies by day.

Psalm 91:5

Excerpt from My Diary

Below is an excerpts from my journal two years ago. I thought it would be helpful for you to read where I was and how I am now by answering the questions I had at that time. I believe as "all things are possible with God" Mark 10:27. Psalm 73:23-24 promises, "Yet I am always with you; you hold me by my right hand. You guide me with my counsel, and afterward you will take me into glory." If you are where I was, be patient. It does get better. You can integrate yourself and your anxiety into a workable person.

It is July 4th, 2007. The day of our nation's independence, celebrated for over 200 years. A day celebrated with a lighted sky of sunbursts of varying colors. A day that family and friends get together for great barbeques and festivities. A day that laughter fills the void between the firework *oohs* and *aahs*. A day I have fond memories of in my distant past. A day just a year ago was a reprieve from the "bombs bursting in air," a day of hope for the future. Could today be the day that I gain my independence from my own void of life? I awoke after a much disrupted sleep and began to prepare for the day. My husband called which is the highlight of each day even though our communication has been reduced to "how I am feeling".

I struggle to get out of bed. Some days this may take till noon due to exhaustion, fears, depression and loss of hope. Other days I get up only to return to my bed for the day, as even the living room poses a threat I don't have the strength to face. The hope I have lost is internal, as at this time in my life I don't live in the outside world, but exist in the pseudo life I have created. I sit in the bed and think about the day, as I have to have a plan to get through each hour. I vaguely remember my life prior to this invasion. I planned my day then also, though vastly different. Today I have to have some safeguards against the sounds that will come with the fireworks display, which I feel the world will enjoy and yet I remain petrified and alone. My parent's will be here with me as part of my plan.

The last month I have thought that my family, especially my husband would be better off without my problems, and I have thought how to end my life that would be least disruptive for them. I spoke to my husband about the plans recently and was immediately filled with regret because of the concern I heard in his voice, and I knew that I am causing pain to those I love. I feel I'm in a no-win situation, and I cannot even gauge who is safe and who is not. I know we live in the U.S. and it is said to be the greatest country on earth, the home of the free, but I am a prisoner, not "feeling" the freedom that is spoken of. Who is the captor? I cannot rationalize it, as it appears that it is I, my thoughts, my feelings and reactions.

It is now 5PM, I don't know where the day has gone. Much of the time I move through a fog, and at others times I just prepare. To prepare against a threat in the past is a very taxing feat and one I have difficulty with daily. How does one prepare against a past threat? Today I will take medication an hour early, preparing for dusk, when the noises may startle me or my thoughts terrify me. What a choice one has. Beyond that I will speak to the love of my life and pretend all is well, talking about the weather, the cat, children, anything except about my existence. I try to be in the moment for him and sometimes it helps when he talks about his trials and I can pretend to be my old self.

That is enough to keep my anxiety hopefully at a productive level without overwhelming my mind, or a more apt possibility, my mind from overwhelming me. Sometimes the flashback is so vivid I cannot bring myself to separate from the intensity of the feelings. I have yet accomplished the ability to separate myself from the terror but have become a pro at separating myself from the moments of each day. Is that why I do not feel I live in the same world as others? Is my world so stagnant that I cannot smell the freshness that each new adventure brings? I would have to say yes as I find fear versus adventure, and that is depressing in a way that words do not express justly.

I know in my intelligent being that I am not alone in my feelings or the challenges that I endure, but on an emotional level I cannot find a connectedness to the world that continues without me. I believe that is some of the loss I feel, that the world continues while I stand still.

If I could paint, I would paint myself out of my existence and into the life full of colors of hope, joy, and love, and I would live there with my loved ones - or at the very least bring those colors to their lives.

It is time for medications a statement I would never have imagined saying in my "previous life." Do I depend on them too much? Are they helping? How do I know? On what basis am I making or not making progress, which some would argue is making decisions that are in my best interests? Whom do I trust to be able to provide me the accurate feedback I need? Maybe I will again someday enjoy the festivities of the day.

As I re-read this entry into my journal, I do not recognize that person. I can see how much God has done in my life. I have integrated my anxiety into my life so that I do feel some control over my emotions.

If you recognized yourself in my journal entry, have faith in God that you, too, can come to feel as a whole person with joy and happiness in your life. I am reminded of a scripture in John where Jesus describes himself as a vine and we are the branches. As we remain connected to him, we will live and bear fruit (John 15:4). I may have let go of the vine, but God did not let go of me. He carried me through the roughest of times.

Try journaling all your fears and anxieties, including the associated feelings. Take a moment each day to re-read what you have written and see if you, too, can notice where God has intervened in your life, moments and events where the fears were not realized but remained as fears. A journal is a safe way to present all your fears and anxieties up to the LORD, even though he already knows what is in your heart.

(Say) to those with fearful hearts,

"Be strong, do not fear;

your God will come,…"

Isaiah 35:4

Anniversary Reactions

God tells us to be strong because our strength comes from him and do not fear because he is with us. "All the days of hard service, I will wait for my renewal to come" (Job 14:14). Our renewal will come in its own time. Anniversaries occur every day. Some are happy (weddings, new jobs, and birthdays), and some are sad and bring up painful memories (death, traumatic events, divorces). We celebrate some and mourn others. If your anxiety is from a traumatic event, you may notice that around that time of year or day that your symptoms become worse. That is normal and is something you can work on. The intensity of these reactions will lessen over time.

Plan for the anniversary. Include your family, and let them know that this will be a difficult time for you. Plan to include some quiet time for reflection, prayer, and meditation. Make your schedule light so you are not overly stressed, but include something you enjoy, something that will bring you peace. In John 14:27, Jesus said, " Peace I leave with you; my peace I give you. I do not give as the world gives. Do not let your hearts be troubled and do not be afraid."

Some symptoms you may experience include;

Cognitive	Emotional	Physical
Confusion	moodiness	fatigue
Forgetfulness	irritability	muscle tension
Nightmares	emotional numbing	increased heart rate
Self-blame	vulnerability	nausea

This is not an all-inclusive list. If the symptoms are severe, please contact your doctor.

Below is a stretching exercise from my chiropractor that stretches your back, legs, arms, and neck. This is a good exercise to practice when you are coping with a sad anniversary.

1. Get on all fours, with your arms beneath your shoulders and your knees beneath your hips.

2. Use your abdominal muscles and round your back and relax your neck.
3. Inhale and relax your spine into your body. Complete this five times. Then come to a neutral spine (your spine should be level with your shoulders and hips).
4. Extend your right arm to shoulder height and left leg to hip height. Stretch and release.
5. Extend your left arm and right leg as above. Stretch and release. Complete ten times.

But because of his great love for us,

God, who is rich in mercy, made us

alive with Christ even when we were

dead in transgressions - it is by grace

you have been saved.

Ephesians 2: 4-5

Assistance Dogs

If you look back over your life, you can find many obstacles that you have overcome and that you did not battle alone. In many instances it was by the grace of God you were spared any further injuries or pain. God's love for us sustains us in times of trials, and we never have to fear because he will never leave us. He even sent his Son to the world of sin to give us everlasting life.

One of the interesting facts I have found in my research is that mental disorders fall under the Americans with Disabilities Act and in many cases qualify you for a service dog. If you have a dog of your own, you can train it to be a service dog and it can go with you into any public building as long as you have had the training documented, the dog passes certain skills, you have a note from your doctor stating you need a service dog for anxiety, the dog is not a harm to the public, and it has the colored vest identifying it as a service dog. The Goldstar German Shepherd Web site (http://goldstargermanshepherds. com) sells training CD's and vests for your dog.

If you think a service dog can assist you in getting out into the public more and feel safe, then I recommend you check out the Web site. If you are not a dog person, try a cat, which can provide comfort and relaxation. Research shows that blood pressure goes down while rubbing an animal or watching fish swim. During times of anxiety our heart rate goes up, so whatever we can do to keep it at a normal level is good for our health.

God made all the things on earth for us - the flowers, the grass, the animals - and he will provide for them. Psalm 145:15-16 says, "The eyes of all look to you, and you give them their food at the proper time. You open your hand and satisfy the desires of every living thing."

Find something living that you can care for that will help deflect your focus from your anxiety. If not an animal, choose a plant, something that requires you to care for it and something you can find enjoyment in.

If it is possible, as far as it depends on you,

live at peace with everyone.

Romans 12:18

Sometimes They Are Just Accidents

Living in peace sounds so easy in writing, but in reality it is difficult to accomplish. God gives us his examples of living in love and peace; for example ""the LORD make his face shine upon you and be gracious to you; the LORD turn his face toward you and give you peace." (Numbers 7:25-26). His support to you can be found in Psalm 145:17 "The LORD is righteous in all his ways and loving toward all He has made". We worked on forgiveness earlier in the book as a form of freedom for you. Now take that a step further and try to live in peace and accept accidents do happen.

I was in an automobile accident that wasn't my fault, but I suffered an anxiety attack at the hospital and then had a flashback. It was a terrible time for me, and I know it wasn't easy on the staff caring for me. However, they treated me with kindness and concern, never judging but always encouraging me. This was another time when God worked through others to show his love and tenderness towards me.

I could have chosen to be angry at the other driver for my spiral downward, but I was able to recognize it as an accident and not an intentional deed. Furthermore, the hospital staff could have become frustrated at me and refused to treat me or had me committed, but they remained patient and waited for the flashback to subside.

There may be times when you are angry about a situation that was caused by someone else, but consider what you would gain, or more important what you would lose. Accidents are just that and sometimes are unpreventable. This is not a time to become angry and risk losing your control. You will gain much confidence in controlling yourself and a peace in knowing that you can control your reactions. You may become angry and then pray about it and find that it is not worth your anger. Letting God hold your hand you apologize for any outbursts. You will be surprised at the relief you'll have by letting go of the anger. That's what God does. "Who is a God like you, who pardons sin and forgives the transgression of the remnant of his inheritance? You do not stay angry forever but delight to show mercy" (Mic. 7:18).

Losing control, such as, anger is a burden that we carry. Feel the weight of it on your shoulders. Who needs that extra weight when we have a life made perfect in God?

The following exercise is to help you maintain control of your reactions which is a goal in dealing with anxieties.

1. In prayer lift up to the Lord all your anxieties and pray for peace within yourself.
2. Listen with your heart and be patient. Not all your reactions will be lifted easily, but it is worth your peace of mind to be able to live peacefully with others.
3. Write down what you have lifted up and come back to read it in a few days. Watch how God works in helping you live in peace.

Isaiah 53:5 says, "But he was pierced for our transgressions, he was crushed for our iniquities; the punishment that brought us peace was upon him and by his wounds we were healed."

Our anxieties may stay with us, but the severity may lessen as we find effective means of coping and living a full and fulfilling, joyful live with our illness.

In my anguish I cried to the LORD and

he answered by setting me free.

The LORD is with me; I will not be afraid.

Psalm 118:5-6

Delusional Thinking

In anxiety, fear is a common emotion we must deal with. Difficulty concentrating or delusional thinking also occur in some anxiety disorders. These, too, can be lessened with practice and grounding exercises.

Delusions are fixed beliefs with some basis in reality. Delusional thinking can lead to anxiety and paranoia due to a loss of touch of reality. It is essential that you have a safety plan in place with phone numbers to friends, family, and health care providers for the family, as well as, for yourself. It is not enough for someone to tell you that something is not real. You have to work through delusions with grounding, relaxation skills, a hobby, journaling, or meditation.

My brain can come up with some unsafe feelings even when I am literally safe. I breathe and ground myself by looking around and noticing things that are familiar and safe.

You can do the same. Name your safe and familiar tings; your couch, your home, your painting, etc . If you are out in public, go to your car and name things in your car that are familiar until you are comfortable calming yourself in public places. I mentally or physically go to my safe place, but that takes time and practice to go to your safe place mentally.

The LORD has set me free, I am more in control of my anxiety reactions than I was three years ago, but at times I am caught off guard and use my confidant to help me get back to my reality. James 1:17 says, "Every good and perfect gift is from above, coming down from the Father of the heavenly lights." I try to remember this; I was given good gifts here on earth from my husband, family, friends, and life. I try to live my life pleasing to God's eyes even with my anxiety.

The following is a meditation to help you focus on the "Here and Now."

1. Sit or lie comfortably. Close your eyes and focus on your breathing. Come to a relaxed state.
2. Visualize that you are walking through a forest with trees so thick that they block out the sunlight, but you know God is walking with you, so you keep traveling.

3. You come to lush, green meadows filled with daisies and sunlight. You are lying there, God is with you, and you feel the warmth from the sun penetrating your mind and body.
4. Imagine the warmth talking to you and telling you to relax; the heat traveling through your body. Lie there as long as you want.

An angel from heaven appeared to
him and strengthened him. And being
in anguish, he prayed more earnestly,
and his sweat was like drops of blood
falling to the ground.

Luke 22:43-44

Self-confidence and Self-esteem

We all need strength and support, and that is what God offers - and more. His love is abounding and encircles you and holds you close.   First John 4:16-17 says, "And so we know and rely on the love God has for us. God is love. Whoever lives in love lives in God, and God in him. In this way, love is made complete among us so that we will have confidence on the day of judgment."

With anxiety you may lack confidence or self-esteem. You may not feel you are "enough." God comes to us where we are; he does not expect us to be perfect, just pleasing to Him.

My self-confidence was shattered when I felt I no longer had control of my life, but that is where God wants us. In our brokenness our spirit can be lifted up to God and he can to be our guide in living life. It takes courage to live with an anxiety disorder, and that is what you are doing.

Self-confidence is having confidence in you. Self-esteem is a value or pride in oneself. I volunteer which increases my self-confidence and self-esteem, it also gives back to the community. You can't buy love, support, self-esteem, and self-confidence.   I had a very low self-worth because I was unable to do the job I loved and trained for in the way that I was accustomed. However, I have found that volunteering is flexible and self-fulfilling.

Some of what we say to ourselves contributes to or diminishes from our self-confidence. If you use positive self-talk and recognize your accomplishments no matter how small, it will boost your self-confidence. If your self-worth is negative talk with your confidant or your counselor or doctor. A negative self-worth can lead to serious consequences.

To help you identify the accomplishments you make each day, complete the following exercise.

1.   Write down all that you accomplish in a day; include all the little things you may not feel are important.   For example, it may be that you got out of the house and walked to the mailbox or created a wonderful meal.
2.   Read it at the end of the day and thank God that you accomplished those things.

3. Make a list of realistic accomplishments you want to achieve and pray about them.
4. Work slowly, remember to be patient, and review your progress periodically.
5. Develop a hobby, if you do not already have one, such as cooking, gardening, writing, painting or participating in a sport. You will be surprised how relaxing and satisfying a hobby can be.

But you, O LORD, are a compassionate

and gracious God, slow to anger,

abounding in love and faithfulness.

Psalm 86:15

Phobias

Phobias come in a variety of intensity and in diagnosis. They disrupt our lives and cause us anxiety and/or panic attacks. They interfere with our social and personal lives, including our relationships with loved ones. They interrupt our ability to identify the truth in situations. John 14:16-17 Jesus says, "And I will ask the Father, and he will give you another Counselor to be with you forever- the Spirit of truth."

One method in treating phobias is Systematic Desensitization. It is where small systemized steps are taken to desensitize someone to a phobia. If you are in counseling, your counselor may be using this technique with you in session. I will use my own experience to work through this technique.

I had a phobia of driving after an incident in Kuwait. To overcome this phobia, first I had my husband drive me as I got use to being in the car. Next, I just sat in my vehicle and imagined driving to work. Then I sat in my car and started it and tuned the radio to a station I enjoyed. Next, I drove around my housing addition. Then I visualized myself driving to work and focused on my breathing. This took time to accomplish. I still sometimes have panic attacks, and when I do, I do breathing exercises.

Panic attacks and severe stress can cause muscle tension. Here is a stretch I use for my entire body and to rejuvenate my brain.

1. Begin by getting on your hands and knees with your arms slightly in front of your shoulders.
2. Raise up on your hands and the balls of your feet, with your knees slightly bent.
3. Push your body back into the balls of your feet.
4. Feel the stretch in your legs and arms. Your spine and neck should be relaxed.
5. Hold for about thirty seconds.

Let the morning bring me word of
your unfailing love, for I have put my
trust in you. Show me the way I should
go, for to you I lift up my soul.

Psalm 143:8

Guilt

With each morning come new hope, desires, and events. Show me the way, LORD, for I am troubled, and all the answers to life's questions lie in your hand. I trust you to light my path. Jeremiah 17:14 says, "Heal me, O LORD and I will be healed; save me and I will be saved, for you are the one I praise." God has a plan for each of us.

Guilt is often a product of or a contributing factor to an anxiety disorder. This is true in sexual trauma, PTSD, and other anxiety disorders. We may be full of "what ifs" or "If I had or had not". We may be filled with guilt over our actions or comments that we made to someone when our anxiety was at an intolerable limit.

Take your guilt to God. He can restore your joy. As Psalm 51:12 says, Restore to me the joy of your salvation and grant me a willing spirit, to sustain me." David wrote that psalm after repenting of his transgressions.

You can always take your guilt to God, but it is also necessary that you share it with your confidant, even if it will make you vulnerable. Vulnerability comes when we share something we are ashamed of or that we think someone will judge us for. Sharing our guilt takes trust.

In sharing you'll have to rely on the integrity, strength, and ability, in your confidant. This may be difficult, but if you can trust that person, you'll be able to share honestly from your heart and mind what is going on with you at any given moment.

It may take time for you to share your thoughts and feelings with another person. Be patient. and in the meantime take your feelings to God. God is our comforter. He will never think less of you. He accepts and loves you where you are at any given moment.

Honor yourself by relieving yourself of the burden of guilt it is excess baggage you haven't earned or deserve. The following exercise will help the tension that guilt can have on the body.

1. Stand with your feet hips-width apart.
2. Stretch your arms overhead and reach for the sky. Pull your ribs away from your waist.

3. Bend from your hips and place your hands on your shins, ankles, or the floor
3. Breathe calmly.
4. Relax your spine and neck; hold for about thirty seconds.
5. Reach your hands back over your head.

For great is his love toward us,

and the faithfulness of the LORD

endures forever. Praise the LORD.

Psalm 117:2

Confusion

God's love surrounds you and comforts you. He is always faithful in his covenant with you. This is for eternity. "For we are God's workmanship, created in Christ Jesus to do good works, which God prepared in advance for us to do." (Eph. 2:10). God created you for a purpose. He has a plan for you, but it is still up to you to use the gifts he gave you for good. This may be taking care of your family, volunteering, or being a good friend. "We have different gifts, according to the grace given us." (Rom. 12:6).

Your days may be hectic; you may get confused, easily distracted, or lose time. Have you ever gone to the store only to be too anxious to remember what you went in there for? Or maybe you have forgotten an appointment that you had. Confusion can be triggered by anxiety.

Confusion may lead to communication problems with others because you are not getting a point across in an understandable way. Try deep breathing, slowly in and out through your nose, feeling the rise in your chest. Grounding is also useful; look around and name things in your head that you see, that can get you back to the "Here and Now". If you have a spouse and he or she thinks you are confused, educate your spouse to ask you where your head is at in such moments. It will open up communication and you will become aware of where your thoughts are.

Organization is key to combat moments of confusion brought on by anxiety. You can do simple things to stay organized. Keep items in a specific place so you can find them without frustration. Use a calendar to keep track of appointments and events. Make a list prior to going to the store, preferably the day before. I have learned that lists and calendars are an important part of my life.

Take your mind off you confusion by focusing on the following physical exercise.

1. Lie on your stomach on the floor with your arms above your head.
2. Raise your right arm and left leg, your head should follow the arc of your spine. Release.
3. Raise your left arm and right leg then release.
4. Repeat 10 times.

I pray your journey to whole-health wellness is filled with little joys and delights. "Our mouths were filled with laughter, our tongues with songs of joy" (Ps. 126:2-3). "The LORD has done great things for us, and we are filled with joy" (Ps. 126:2-3).

If you have any questions about the content of this book you can e-mail me at candccounseling @aol.com. I am going to leave you with my favorite scriptures, and I hope you treat yourself as described.

> *"Love is patient, love is kind. It does not envy, it does not boast, it is not proud. It is not rude, it is not self-seeking, it is not easily angered, it keeps no record of wrongs. Love does not delight in evil, but rejoices with the truth. It always protects, always trusts, always hopes, always perseveres. Love never fails"*

1 Corinthians 13:4-8

Suggested Resources

Here are some helpful Web sites to read or share with family and friends.

David Baldwin's pages Gift from Within are excellent for PTSD sufferers. You can sign up to have someone to e-mail about symptoms, during bad days and utilize the resources available.

Anxiety Disorders Association of America, http://www.adaa.org.

Generalized Anxiety Disorder Information, **Error! Hyperlink reference not valid.**

National Institutes of Health. http://www.nimh.nih.gov. Under Health and Outreach, click Anxiety

National Mental Health Information Center. http://mentalhealth.samhsa.gov/publications/allpubs/ken98-0045/

Post-Traumatic Stress Disorder. http://www.nlm.nih.gov/medlineplus/posttraumaticstressdisorder.html

Gift from Within. http://www.giftfromwithin.org.

Social Anxiety. http://www.socialanxiety.us

Obsessive-Compulsive Disorder http://www.mayoclinic.com/health/obsessive-compulsive-disorder/DS00189

Post-Traumatic Stress Disorder, Symptoms and Resourceshttp://www.veteransfamiliesunited.org/Post-TraumaticStressDisorderSymptomsandResources.html

Phobias. http://www.mayoclinic.com/health/phobias/DS00272/DSECTION=symptoms

Bibliography

Brantley, Jeffrey, and Millstine, Wendy. *Daily meditations for calming your anxious mind.* New Harbinger Publications: Oakland, Calif. 2008.

Central Mass Yoga Institute. *Yoga, Post-Traumatic Stress Disorder and the Mind Body.* http://www.centralmassyoga.com/ptsd.htm

Corey, Gerald. *Theory and Practice of Counseling and Psychotherapy,* 5th ed. Brooks/Cole Publishing Company: Belmont, Calif. 1996.

Diagnostic and Statistical Manual of Mental Disorders 4th ed. American Psychiatric Association: Arlington, Va.

Figley, Charles and Nash, William, eds. *Combat Stress Injury: Theory, Research, and Management.* Routledge, London 2006.

Shin, Lisa and Handwerger, Kathryn. " *Is Posttraumatic Stress Disorder a Stress-Induced Fear Circuitry Disorder?".* Journal of Traumatic Stress 22 no. 5 (2009).

Kelly, Eugene W., Jr. Spirituality and Religion in Counseling and Psychotherapy: Diversity in Theory and Practice. American Counseling Association: Alexandria, Va., 1995.

van der Kolk, Bessel. *"The Body Keeps Score: Memory and the Evolving Psychobiology of Post-Traumatic Stress."* Harvard Review of Psychiatry

1 no. 5 (1994)

Walters, Sheryl. *"Utilize Yoga to Help Heal Posttraumatic Stress Disorder."* Natural News. May 5 2009, http://www.naturalnews.com/026201.html.

Teressa "Jazz" Huff-Garrett resides in southern Oklahoma with her husband, Billy Garrett. She has two grown children, Jason and Brandy, and five grandchildren. Teressa graduated from Mary Hardin-Baylor and Northwestern Oklahoma State University. She has been working with anxiety disorders on both a small and large scale for more than twelve years. Teressa is a Licensed Professional Counselor, Certified Traumatologist, Life Coach, speaker and business owner. She counseled survivors at the Oklahoma City bombing and the 9-11 terrorist attacks. She also spent twenty-six months counseling traumatized and anxious persons in Iraq, Kuwait, and Afghanistan from 2004 to 2006. She volunteers as the Mental Health Lead at the Texoma Chapter of the American Red Cross, where she works on local and national disasters and provides training to new counselors.